I dedicate this to my mother. Thank you for turing me into the man I am.

SINCERELY, CHRIS

TABLE OF CONTENTS

ANCIENT CIVILIZATIONS   1-20

- *Egypt: Pyramids, Pharaohs, and the Nile*
- *Mesopotamia: Cradle of Civilization*
- *Indus Valley: Mysterious Beginnings*
- *Ancient China: Dynasties and Innovations*
- *Mesoamerica: Mayans, Aztecs, and Incas*

GREAT EMPIRES AND KINGDOMS   21-38

- *Roman Empire: Conquests and Culture*
- *Persian Empire: A Story of Power*
- *Mongol Empire: Genghis Khan's Legacy*
- *Ottoman Empire: Crossroads of Cultures*
- *British Empire: Sun Never Set*

WORLD MYSTERIES   39-51

- Crop Circles
- Stonehenge
- Easter Island
- Strange inventions
- Wacky Locations

CULTURAL AND SCIENTIFIC ACHIEVEMENTS   52-67

- *Renaissance: Rebirth of Art and Knowledge*
- *Scientific Revolution: Changing Views of the Universe*
- *Industrial Revolution: Transformation of Societies*
- *Digital Revolution: The Information Age*

TABLE OF CONTENTS

WARS AND CONFLICTS   68-87

- The American Revolutionary War
- The Napoleonic Wars
- World War I: The Great War
- World War II: A Global Struggle
- Cold War: Ideological Showdown

RELIGIONS AND MYTHOLOGY   88-107

- African Mythologies
- Greek Mythology
- Hinduism
- Buddhism
- Aztec Mythology:
- Aboriginal Australian Myths
- Zoroastrianism

USELESS AND RANDOM INFO   108-125

- The Lost City of Atlantis: Myth or Reality?
- The Knights of the Round Table
- The Black Death: A Historical Pandemic
- Marco Polo
- The Mystery of Roanoke Island
- Vlad the Impaler
- The Wright Brothers
- The Great Emu War

01

CHAPTER

ANCIENT EGYPT

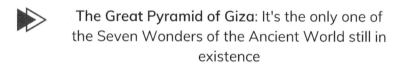

SO WHATS THE BIG DEAL ANYWAY?

▷▷ **The Great Pyramid of Giza**: It's the only one of the Seven Wonders of the Ancient World still in existence

▷▷ Hieroglyphics: Ancient Egyptians used more than 700 hieroglyphs, a complex writing system that combined logographic and alphabetic elements.

▷▷ The Rosetta Stone: Discovered in 1799, this granodiorite stele was key in deciphering Egyptian hieroglyphs, thanks to its inscriptions in three scripts.

▷▷ Mummification: This process was not just for preserving the dead; it was crucial for ensuring a safe passage to the afterlife.

▷▷ Cats: Revered in Ancient Egypt, cats were considered sacred and were often mummified and buried with their owners.

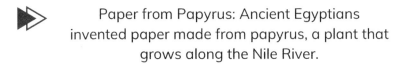

▶▶ Paper from Papyrus: Ancient Egyptians invented paper made from papyrus, a plant that grows along the Nile River.

▶▶ **The Calendar**: They developed a calendar based on the lunar and solar cycles, remarkably similar to the one we use today.

▶▶ Medical Knowledge: They practiced advanced medicine and surgery, with evidence of brain surgery dating back to 3000 BC.

▶▶ The Sphinx: The Great Sphinx of Giza, with a lion's body and a human head, is one of the largest and oldest statues in the world.

▶▶ Children's Games: Ancient Egyptian children played with toys like dolls, miniature houses, and board games like Senet.

▶▶ Beer and Bread: These were staples in the Egyptian diet, with beer being consumed daily by people of all ages, including children.

Cosmetics: Both men and women wore makeup, not only for aesthetics but also for health reasons, as it protected their skin from the sun.

 Nile River: Ancient Egypt's civilization flourished around the Nile, relying on its annual floods for agriculture.

 The Book of the Dead: This is not a single book but a collection of spells and instructions to guide the deceased through the underworld.

 Lengthy Process: Mummification took about 70 days to complete. The body was washed, organs were removed, and the body was filled with spices and wrapped in linen.

 Artificial Eyes: Sometimes artificial eyes were placed in the mummy's sockets to make them appear more lifelike.

 Animal Mummies: Not just humans, but also animals like cats, dogs, crocodiles, and birds were mummified.

 Animal Mummies: Not just humans, but also animals like cats, dogs, crocodiles, and birds were mummified.

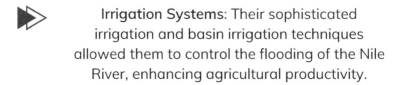 **Irrigation Systems**: Their sophisticated irrigation and basin irrigation techniques allowed them to control the flooding of the Nile River, enhancing agricultural productivity.

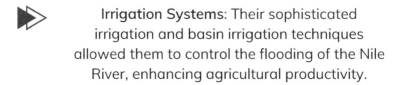 Mathematics: Egyptians made significant advances in mathematics, particularly in geometry, necessary for building their architectural wonders.

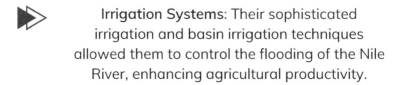 Medicine: They were pioneers in medicine, with medical practices recorded on various papyri showing advanced understanding of anatomy and healthcare.

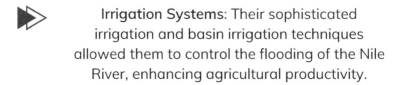 Shipbuilding: Ancient Egyptians were adept shipbuilders, creating seaworthy vessels that facilitated trade and travel across the Nile and beyond.

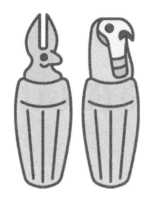

▷▷ **Honey as a Sweetener and Preservative**: They used honey extensively, not just as a sweetener but also for its preservative and antibacterial properties. Honey found in ancient tombs is still edible today.

▷▷ Shaving Eyebrows for Cats: When a family cat died, all members of the household would shave their eyebrows in mourning.

▷▷ Servants Covered in Honey: To keep flies away from the pharaoh, some servants were smeared with honey to attract the flies to themselves instead of the pharaoh.

▷▷ Dentistry: They had dental problems due to the grit and sand in their diet. Some mummies have been found with dental work, including primitive but effective tooth fillings.

▷▷ The First Labor Strike in History: Recorded around 1170 BC, workers at the royal necropolis at Deir el-Medina walked off the job because they had not been paid.

MESOPOTAMIA:

WHERE DID SOCIETY START AGAIN?

 Name Origin: Mesopotamia means "between rivers" in Greek, referring to its location between the Tigris and Euphrates rivers.

 First Cities: It's home to some of the first known cities, like Uruk, Ur, and Eridu.

 Cuneiform Writing: The world's oldest known writing system, cuneiform, originated in Mesopotamia around 3200 BCE.

 The Wheel: The wheel was invented in Mesopotamia around 3500 BCE, initially used for pottery.

 Ziggurats: These massive terraced temples were central to many Mesopotamian cities.

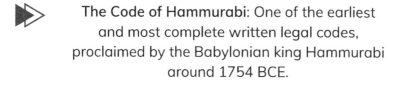

▶▷ **The Code of Hammurabi:** One of the earliest and most complete written legal codes, proclaimed by the Babylonian king Hammurabi around 1754 BCE.

▶▷ Epic of Gilgamesh: One of the earliest great works of literature, originating from ancient Mesopotamia.

▶▷ Mathematics: The Mesopotamians developed a base-60 number system, which is why we have 60 seconds in a minute and 360 degrees in a circle.

▶▷ Astronomy and Astrology: They made significant contributions to the field of astronomy and also practiced astrology, believing celestial bodies influenced their daily lives.

▶▷ The Hanging Gardens of Babylon: One of the Seven Wonders of the Ancient World, although their existence remains a topic of debate.

Babylon: An ancient city famous for its opulence and the Tower of Babel, which was likely a ziggurat.

 Glassmaking: Mesopotamia was one of the first regions to produce glass and glassware.

 Seals and Signatures: They used cylinder seals to roll an impression on wet clay, which acted as a signature for documents and goods.

 Lion Hunt Relief Sculptures: Assyrian kings celebrated their power through reliefs depicting lion hunts, seen as a symbol of the king's might.

 Schools: They had a type of school known as an edubba where scribes were trained.

 First Empire: The Akkadian Empire, formed by Sargon of Akkad, is often considered the world's first empire.

 Laws on Women and Marriage: The Mesopotamian marriage contract laws were detailed, including provisions for divorce.

▶▶ **Chariots**: Mesopotamians were among the first to use chariots in warfare.

Polytheistic Religion: Their religion was polytheistic, with gods like Anu, Enlil, and Ishtar.

▶▶ **Social Classes**: Mesopotamian society was stratified, with kings and priests at the top and slaves at the bottom.

▶▶ River of Death: The Tigris and Euphrates rivers were prone to unpredictable and destructive flooding, often wiping out crops and causing famine.

▶▶ Harsh Punishments: The Code of Hammurabi included severe punishments, like cutting off a thief's fingers or gouging out the eyes of a judge who made a wrong decision.

 Marriage Practices: Marriages were often arranged by parents, and bride-price (gifts or money given to the bride's family) was a common practice. Love poems and songs suggest that romantic love was also valued.

 Education and Scribe Schools: Only boys from wealthy families received education, typically aimed at becoming a scribe. This education was rigorous, focusing on learning cuneiform writing and various subjects like mathematics, law, and religion.

 Role of Women: Women in Mesopotamia could own property, run businesses, and were sometimes involved in court cases. However, their primary roles were as wives and mothers, and they had less legal status compared to men.

 Food and Cuisine: The Mesopotamian diet consisted mainly of barley, with beer being a staple beverage. They also ate onions, leeks, garlic, lentils, beans, cucumbers, dates, apples, and a variety of meats, including pork, mutton, beef, and poultry.

Indus Valley

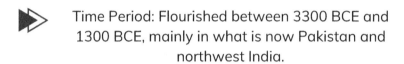

▶▶ Time Period: Flourished between 3300 BCE and 1300 BCE, mainly in what is now Pakistan and northwest India.

▶▶ Undeciphered Script: The Indus script, found on seals and pottery, remains undeciphered to this day.

▶▶ Trade Networks: The civilization had extensive trade relations with Mesopotamia and other regions, evident from the discovery of Indus artifacts in those areas.

▶▶ No Known Rulers: Unlike other ancient civilizations, there is no evidence of any kings, armies, or palaces, suggesting a possibly egalitarian society.

▶▶ Standardized Weights and Measures: Their system of standardized weights and measures indicates a high level of sophistication in trade and economic organization.

▶▶ **Docks and Harbors**: Lothal is believed to have had the world's first known dock, indicating advanced maritime trade.

▶▶ No Large Monuments: Unlike contemporaneous cultures, the Indus Valley Civilization did not build massive monuments or temples.

▶▶ Water Management: They engineered sophisticated water supply and drainage systems, including wells and public baths.

▶▶ Absence of Military Structures: There's little evidence of military activity, suggesting a peaceful society or effective governance systems that prevented conflict.

▶▶ Jewelry and Ornaments: They made sophisticated jewelry from gold, silver, ivory, and precious stones.

ANCIENT CHINA

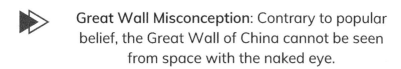

SO MANY INVENTIONS!

▶▷ **Great Wall Misconception**: Contrary to popular belief, the Great Wall of China cannot be seen from space with the naked eye.

▶▷ **Invention of Paper**: Around 105 AD, the Chinese invented paper, revolutionizing the way information was recorded and shared.

▶▷ Gunpowder Discovery: Chinese alchemists accidentally discovered gunpowder while searching for an immortality elixir.

▶▷ Terracotta Army: The Terracotta Army, built for Emperor Qin Shi Huang, contains over 8,000 soldiers, 130 chariots, and 670 horses, all life-sized and unique.

▶▷ Seismograph Innovation: In 132 AD, a Chinese astronomer named Zhang Heng invented the first seismograph, an instrument to detect earthquakes.

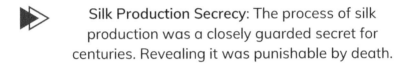 **Silk Production Secrecy**: The process of silk production was a closely guarded secret for centuries. Revealing it was punishable by death.

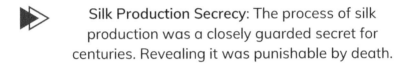 **First Use of Money**: China was the first country in the world to use paper money, during the Tang Dynasty (618-907 AD).

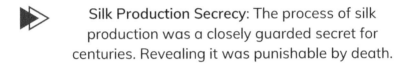 Invention of Printing: The world's first movable type printing technology was developed in China around 1040 AD, predating Gutenberg's press by over 400 years.

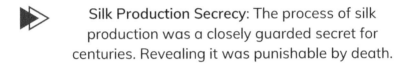 The Forbidden City: The Forbidden City in Beijing contains 9,999 rooms. It was believed that only heaven had 10,000 rooms.

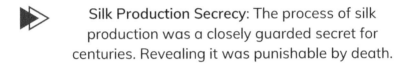 Civil Service Exam: The Chinese established the imperial civil service examination system to select state bureaucrats, a practice that lasted over a millennium.

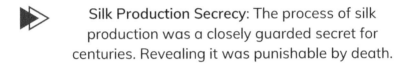 Compass for Navigation: The magnetic compass, a critical navigation tool, was first invented in China during the Han Dynasty.

The Oldest Observatory: The Gaocheng Astronomical Observatory, built in 1276, is one of the oldest observatories in the world.

 Soccer Origin: A game resembling soccer, called Cuju, was popular in ancient China and is considered a precursor to modern soccer.

 Kite Invention: Kites were first created in China for military purposes, such as signaling and measuring distances.

 The Grand Canal: The Grand Canal, constructed during the Sui Dynasty, is the longest canal or artificial river in the world.

 Tea Discovery: According to legend, tea was discovered by Emperor Shen Nong in 2737 BC when tea leaves blew into his boiling water.

 Toilet Paper: China was the first to use paper for hygiene purposes in the 6th century.

 Acupuncture and Traditional Medicine: Acupuncture has been practiced in China for thousands of years, part of a holistic approach to medicine.

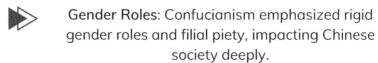 **Gender Roles**: Confucianism emphasized rigid gender roles and filial piety, impacting Chinese society deeply.

Chinese Zodiac: The Chinese zodiac, a 12-year cycle with each year represented by an animal, has ancient origins and plays a significant role in Chinese culture.

Chopsticks: Chopsticks have been used in China for over 3,000 years, originally for cooking and later as eating utensils.

Feng Shui: The practice of Feng Shui, arranging the environment harmoniously, dates back at least 3,500 years in China.

MESO AMERICA

THE STARS. A MYSTERY? I THINK NOT!

 Advanced Astronomy: The Maya had an intricate and accurate calendar system based on astronomical observations.

 Writing System: The Maya developed the only true writing system in the pre-Columbian Americas, known as Maya script.

 Ball Game: They played a game called Pitz, similar to a mix of soccer and basketball, often with religious significance.

 Chocolate Lovers: The Maya were one of the first to cultivate cacao and made a chocolate drink for rituals and as a luxury for the elite.

 End of the World Prediction: The Maya calendar's end in 2012 led to a modern myth about the world ending.

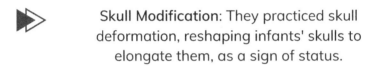

Skull Modification: They practiced skull deformation, reshaping infants' skulls to elongate them, as a sign of status.

Mathematical Concept of Zero: The Maya independently developed the concept of zero around 4 AD.

Architecture: They built impressive structures, including pyramids, without metal tools, the wheel, or draft animals.

Floating Gardens: The Aztecs built chinampas, or floating gardens, for agriculture in Lake Texcoco.

Capital City: Their capital, Tenochtitlan, built on an island in a lake, was one of the largest cities in the world at its height.

Education for All: Both boys and girls received basic education, a rare practice in many ancient societies.

Chocolate Currency: Cacao beans were used as a form of currency.

 Calendar System: Like the Maya, they had a sophisticated calendar system consisting of a 365-day agricultural calendar and a 260-day ritual calendar.

 Warfare and Expansion: Military conquest was central to Aztec culture, with warfare serving as a means of expansion and religious expression.

 Aztec Poetry: They had a rich tradition of poetry, known as "flower and song," which was an important part of their culture.

 Road System: They built an extensive and sophisticated network of roads and bridges across harsh mountain terrains.

 Machu Picchu: This famous mountain city is a testament to Incan architectural skill.

 No Iron or Steel: Despite their architectural feats, they did not use iron or steel.

▶▶ **Terraced Farming**: They used advanced terraced farming techniques to grow crops on steep hillsides.

▶▶ **Unique Tax System**: Citizens paid taxes through labor, contributing to public works and agricultural production.

▶▶ **Child Sacrifice**: The Incas practiced child sacrifice in rituals known as capacocha, particularly during times of famine, epidemics, or the death of an emperor.

▶▶ **Empire of Many Languages**: While Quechua was the administrative language, the empire was home to many languages and ethnic groups.

02

CHAPTER

02

ROMAN EMPIRE

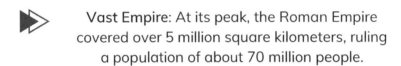

▶▶ **Vast Empire:** At its peak, the Roman Empire covered over 5 million square kilometers, ruling a population of about 70 million people.

▶▶ **Roman Law:** Roman law laid the foundation for many legal systems in Western countries today.

▶▶ **Concrete Innovation:** The Romans were pioneers in using concrete for construction, which enabled them to build structures like the Pantheon.

▶▶ **Road Network:** They built a road network of over 80,000 kilometers, which facilitated trade and military movements.

▶▶ **Aqueducts:** Roman aqueducts, some still in use, were engineering marvels that transported water over long distances.

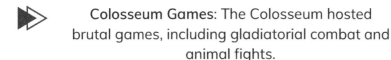

▷▷ **Colosseum Games**: The Colosseum hosted brutal games, including gladiatorial combat and animal fights.

▷▷ **Julius Caesar's Assassination**: In 44 BC, Julius Caesar was assassinated by a group of senators, leading to the end of the Roman Republic and the rise of the Roman Empire

▷▷ **Pompeii's Destruction**: The eruption of Mount Vesuvius in 79 AD buried the city of Pompeii, preserving it under ash for centuries.

▷▷ **Roman Baths**: Public baths were a central part of Roman social life, offering hot and cold baths, sports facilities, and libraries.

▷▷ **Latin Language**: Latin, the language of the Romans, is the root of the Romance languages: Italian, French, Spanish, Portuguese, and Romanian.

▷▷ **Roman Numerals**: The Romans used a numeral system that is still in use in various contexts today.

Calendar Reform: Julius Caesar reformed the calendar, creating the Julian calendar, the predecessor of the Gregorian calendar used today.

 Vast Network of Trade: Roman trade networks extended to India, China, and Africa, bringing silk, spices, and other luxury goods to Rome.

 Military Might: The Roman legions were known for their discipline, organization, and innovative tactics.

 Christianity: Originally persecuted, Christianity became the state religion under Emperor Constantine in the 4th century.

 Architectural Influence: Roman architectural styles, like the arch, dome, and vault, have influenced buildings worldwide.

 Legal and Political Systems: Many modern legal and political systems have roots in Roman law and governance.

▶▶ **Tourism**: Ancient Roman sites like the Colosseum, Roman Forum, and Pompeii attract millions of tourists yearly.

▶▶ **Latin in Science and Medicine**: Latin terms are widely used in the sciences, particularly in taxonomy and medicine.

▶▶ Roman Cuisine's Influence: Italian cuisine, with dishes like pasta and pizza, has roots in ancient Roman food practices.

▶▶ Preservation of Ancient Texts: Roman efforts in preserving Greek texts have been crucial for the survival of classical knowledge.

ANCIENT PERSIAN EMPIRE

▶▶ **Cyrus the Great's Human Rights:** Cyrus the Great is often credited with creating the first declaration of human rights, known as the Cyrus Cylinder.

▶▶ **Royal Road:** The Persians built the Royal Road, an ancient highway that was over 2,500 kilometers long, facilitating rapid communication throughout the empire.

▶▶ **The Persian Wars:** They fought famous battles against the Greek city-states, including the Battles of Marathon, Thermopylae, and Salamis.

▶▶ **Zoroastrianism:** This was the dominant religion of the Persian Empire, one of the world's oldest monotheistic religions.

▶▶ **Diverse Empire:** The Persian Empire was incredibly diverse, encompassing various peoples and cultures under its rule.

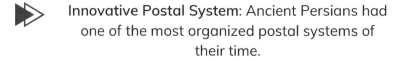

▶▶ **Innovative Postal System**: Ancient Persians had one of the most organized postal systems of their time.

▶▶ **Qanat Water Systems**: They developed an underground canal system called qanat for irrigation, a technology still used in some regions.

▶▶ Achaemenid Architecture: Their architectural style influenced the design of buildings across the empire, including in Egypt and Greece.

▶▶ Persian Language and Literature: Persian poets like Rumi and Hafez have had a lasting impact on literature and poetry.

▶▶ Cyrus's Conquest of Babylon: In 539 BC, Cyrus the Great conquered Babylon, famously doing so without a battle, by diverting the Euphrates River.

▶▶ Immortals: The elite soldiers of the Persian army were known as the Immortals because their number was always kept at exactly 10,000.

Rock Reliefs: The Sassanians created impressive rock reliefs that depicted scenes of royal conquests and ceremonies.

 Revival of Persian Culture: The Sassanian Empire is known for reviving Persian culture and traditions after the Hellenistic influence of the Parthian period.

 Chess Introduction: It's believed that the game of chess, or a precursor to it, originated during the Sassanian period (though some believe it was invented in China or India).

 Academy of Gondishapur: They founded this academy, which became a renowned center of learning in medicine, philosophy, and science.

 Naval Power: They had a significant naval presence, controlling parts of the Persian Gulf and engaging in naval conflicts with Romans.

 Book of Kings (Shahnameh): This epic poem, written much later, glorifies the history of the Persian Empire, including the Sassanians.

THE MONGOL EMPIRE

SO I CAN STILL GET MY MAIL?

 Genghis Khan's Rise: Born as Temujin, Genghis Khan unified the Mongol tribes and launched a series of military campaigns to build the empire.

 Largest Land Empire: At its peak, the Mongol Empire covered over 24 million square kilometers, spanning much of Eurasia.

 Pony Express Style Communication: They established an efficient postal system known as the Yam, with relay stations for fast communication across the empire.

 Religious Tolerance: Genghis Khan and his successors were known for their religious tolerance and often employed people of different faiths.

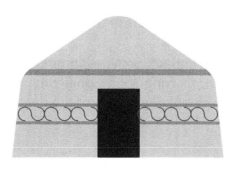

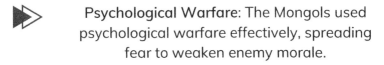

▶▶ **Psychological Warfare**: The Mongols used psychological warfare effectively, spreading fear to weaken enemy morale.

▶▶ **Speed and Mobility**: Their military tactics emphasized speed and mobility, often using feigned retreats to lure enemies into traps.

▶▶ Conquest of Baghdad: In 1258, the Mongols captured Baghdad, marking the end of the Islamic Golden Age.

▶▶ Subutai: One of the greatest Mongol generals, Subutai, led more than 20 campaigns and conquered 32 nations.

▶▶ Legal Code: Genghis Khan established a legal code known as the Yassa, which promoted law and order across the empire.

▶▶ Population Impact: Some estimates suggest that the Mongol conquests significantly reduced the global population at the time.

Descendants: Genghis Khan has millions of living descendants today, as he fathered many children.

 Death in Mystery: The circumstances of Genghis Khan's death remain a mystery, and his burial site has never been found.

 Paper Currency: The Mongols were one of the first to use paper currency extensively throughout the empire.

 Capital Cities: Karakorum and later Khanbaliq (now Beijing) were among the empire's main capitals.

 Marco Polo's Journey: Marco Polo, the Venetian explorer, visited the Mongol Empire and later wrote about his experiences (though some historians believe he lied about almost everything in his stories).

THE OTTOMAN EMPIRE

THEY USED WHAT IN WAR?

 Establishment: The Ottoman Empire was founded around 1299 by Osman I in northwestern Anatolia.

 Longevity: The empire lasted for over 600 years, making it one of the longest-lasting empires in history.

 Vast Territories: At its peak, the empire spanned three continents, controlling much of Southeastern Europe, Western Asia, and Northern Africa.

 Constantinople's Conquest: In 1453, Mehmed the Conqueror seized Constantinople (Istanbul), marking the end of the Byzantine Empire.

 Naval Power: Under Suleiman the Magnificent, the Ottoman navy was a dominant force in the Mediterranean.

▶▶ **Cultural Diversity:** The empire was a melting pot of cultures, religions, and languages due to its vast and diverse territories.

▶▶ The Janissaries: The Janissaries were an elite military unit, originally composed of Christian boys taken from their families, converted to Islam, and trained as soldiers.

▶▶ Architectural Marvels: The Ottomans are famous for their architectural achievements, including the iconic Hagia Sophia and the Blue Mosque.

▶▶ Coffee Culture: The Ottomans popularized coffee drinking, and the first coffee houses in Istanbul became centers of social activity.

▶▶ Language: Ottoman Turkish was the administrative language, which was a mixture of Turkish, Persian, and Arabic.

▶▶ Sultan's Power: The Sultan was the absolute ruler, but his power was often influenced by various court factions and his mother (the Valide Sultan).

33

Legal System: The Ottomans had a complex legal system that included Sharia law and "kanun," or sultanic laws.

 Military Innovations: The Ottomans were pioneers in military technology, including the use of cannons and muskets.

 The Siege of Vienna: The Ottomans famously laid siege to Vienna twice, with the second siege in 1683 marking a turning point leading to the empire's gradual decline in Europe.

 Religious Tolerance: The empire was relatively tolerant of different religions and allowed autonomous communities ("millets") to govern their own affairs.

 Calligraphy and Miniature Painting: The Ottomans were renowned for their art, particularly in calligraphy and miniature painting.

THE BRITTISH EMPIRE

 Largest Empire Ever: At its peak, the British Empire covered over 23% of the world's land surface and governed about 20% of the world's population.

 Sun Never Set: The empire was so widespread that the sun literally never set on it, with colonies in every continent except Antarctica.

 East India Company: Initially a trading entity, it effectively ruled India until control was taken by the British Crown.

 First Colony: The first permanent British colony was established in Jamestown, Virginia, in 1607.

 Languages: English, the language of the British Empire, is now a global language, spoken on every contient on the planet.

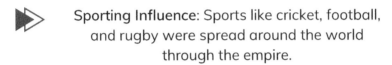 **Sporting Influence:** Sports like cricket, football, and rugby were spread around the world through the empire.

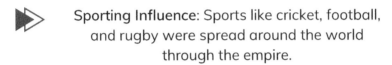 British Tea Culture: Tea, initially imported from China and later grown in India, became a quintessential part of British culture.

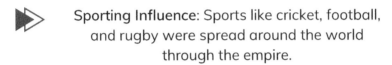 Cultural Exchange: The empire facilitated significant cultural exchanges, influencing literature, art, and music in both the colonies and Britain.

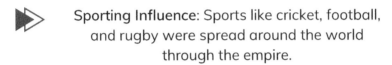 Commonwealth: After decolonization, the British Commonwealth was formed, a political association of former British Empire territories.

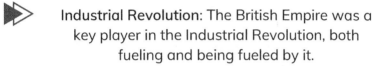 **Industrial Revolution**: The British Empire was a key player in the Industrial Revolution, both fueling and being fueled by it.

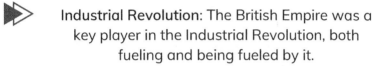 Australia's Colonization: Originally used as a penal colony, Australia's modern development began largely through British convicts sent there.

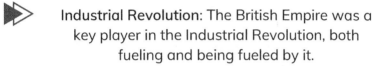 Steam Engine: Invented by James Watt, it was a driving force behind the Industrial Revolution.

Railways: The world's first public railway to use steam locomotives was in Britain.

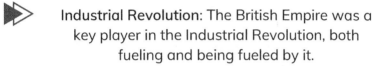 Telephone: Alexander Graham Bell, although born in Scotland, patented the first practical telephone while in Canada, part of the British Empire.

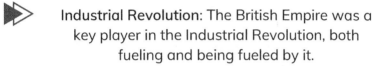 Greenwich Mean Time (GMT): Established in Britain, it became the world standard for timekeeping.

Penicillin: Discovered by Alexander Fleming, a Scotsman, it revolutionized medicine.

 Influence on Education: The British educational model was adopted in almost every part of the world.

 Parliamentary Democracy: The British parliamentary system has influenced many democratic governments in the world and can be found in almost any democratic country.

 Botanic Gardens: The British established botanic gardens in their colonies, like the Royal Botanic Gardens at Kew, to study and exploit plant resources.

 Opium Wars: The British fought the Opium Wars to protect their opium trade in China, leading to the cession of Hong Kong.

03

CHAPTER

03

WORLD MYSTERIES

CROP CIRCLES

 First Documented Instances: The earliest recorded crop circles appeared in the 1600s, with a woodcut from 1678 in Hertfordshire, England, known as the "Mowing-Devil," depicting a strange pattern in a field.

 Increase in Occurrences in the 20th Century: Reports of crop circles became more frequent in the late 20th century, particularly in England, but also in other countries around the world.

 Complex Designs: Early crop circles were simple circular patterns. Over time, they have become increasingly complex, featuring intricate geometric shapes and even three-dimensional effects.

 Made Overnight: Many crop circles are said to appear overnight, often discovered by farmers in the mornings in their fields.

39

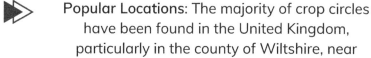

Popular Locations: The majority of crop circles have been found in the United Kingdom, particularly in the county of Wiltshire, near ancient monuments like Stonehenge and Avebury.

Hoaxes and Artistic Expression: In the 1990s, two men from England, Doug Bower and Dave Chorley, claimed responsibility for many crop circles, saying they created them as a form of artistic expression. Since then, many crop circles have been attributed to human artists.

UFO and Paranormal Theories: Some people believe crop circles are created by extraterrestrial beings or are the result of paranormal phenomena. These theories are often bolstered by reports of strange lights or unidentified objects seen in the vicinity of newly formed crop circles.

STONEHENGE

WHY WAS IT BUILT?

 Construction Phases: Stonehenge was built and rebuilt several times over thousands of years. It's earliest construction estimated to be around 5,000 years ago, during the Neolithic period.

 Bluestones: The first stones brought to Stonehenge were the bluestones, which weigh up to 4 tons each and were transported from Wales, about 150 miles away.

 Astronomical Alignments: Stonehenge is aligned with the solstices. Its primary axis is aligned with the sunrise on the summer solstice and the sunset on the winter solstice.

 Burial Site: The area around Stonehenge is one of the densest concentrations of Neolithic and Bronze Age monuments in England, including several hundred burial mounds.

▶▶ **Purpose is Still a Mystery**: The original purpose of Stonehenge is still largely unknown, though theories range from it being a ceremonial site, a religious pilgrimage destination, a final resting place for royalty, or an astronomical observatory.

▶▶ World Heritage Site: In 1986, Stonehenge was added to UNESCO's list of World Heritage Sites, in a co-listing with Avebury, a Neolithic henge located 17 miles away.

▶▶ Modern Celebrations: Stonehenge continues to be an important place of pilgrimage for neo-druids, pagans, and other groups, who celebrate solstices and equinoxes there.

▶▶ Archaeological Research: Ongoing archaeological research and modern scientific techniques continue to shed light on the many unanswered questions about Stonehenge, including how and why it was built.

EASTER ISLAND

HOW MANY STATUES WERE THERE?

▶▶ **Discovery by Europeans**: Easter Island was named by the Dutch explorer Jacob Roggeveen, who first encountered it on Easter Sunday in 1722.

▶▶ Famous for Moai Statues: The island is world-renowned for its 887 monumental statues, called moai, created by the early Rapa Nui people. These statues are carved in the image of ancestral chiefs.

▶▶ Remote Location: Easter Island is one of the world's most isolated inhabited islands, located in the southeastern Pacific Ocean, at the southeasternmost point of the Polynesian Triangle.

▶▶ Annexation by Chile: In 1888, Easter Island was annexed by Chile. The island now has a mixed population, primarily of Polynesian ancestry, along with Chileans from the mainland.

43

 Purpose is Still a Mystery: The original purpose of Stonehenge is still largely unknown, though theories range from it being a ceremonial site, a religious pilgrimage destination, a final resting place for royalty, or an astronomical observatory.

 World Heritage Site: In 1986, Stonehenge was added to UNESCO's list of World Heritage Sites, in a co-listing with Avebury, a Neolithic henge located 17 miles away.

 Modern Celebrations: Stonehenge continues to be an important place of pilgrimage for neo-druids, pagans, and other groups, who celebrate solstices and equinoxes there.

 Archaeological Research: Ongoing archaeological research and modern scientific techniques continue to shed light on the many unanswered questions about Stonehenge, including how and why it was built.

STRANGE INVENTIONS

NO! THAT COULDN'T BE RIGHT??? COULD IT???

Antikythera Mechanism
Use: Ancient astronomical calculator for tracking planetary positions and predicting solar and lunar eclipses.
Inventors: Likely Greek scientists, possibly linked to Archimedes.
Modern Findings: Discovered in a shipwreck off the Greek island of Antikythera in 1901.
Significance: Earliest known analogue computer, showcasing advanced ancient Greek engineering.

Baghdad Battery
Use: Hypothesized to have been used for electroplating or as a galvanic cell.
Inventors: Unknown; discovered in modern-day Iraq and dated to the Parthian period (250 BC – 224 AD).
Modern Findings: Consists of a clay pot, a copper cylinder, and an iron rod.
Speculations: Alternative theories suggest it might have been used for religious rituals involving electric shock.
Significance: Challenges the conventional timeline of the discovery of electricity.

Greek Fire

Use: Incendiary weapon used in naval warfare to set enemy ships ablaze.

Inventors: Credited to the Byzantine Empire, specifically to a Syrian engineer named Callinicus.

Modern Findings: Exact composition remains unknown; believed to have been a petroleum-based mixture.

Speculations: Some suggest additives like quicklime or sulfur were included.

Significance: Provided the Byzantines a significant military advantage, especially at sea.

Damascus Steel

Use: Forged into swords known for their strength, resilience, and distinctive patterns.

Inventors: Originated in the Near East; exact techniques were closely guarded secrets.

Modern Findings: Characterized by the presence of carbon nanotubes and nanowires.

Speculations: The unique properties might be due to the use of specific ores or forging techniques.

Significance: Lost art; modern metallurgists are still trying to replicate its properties.

The Coso Artifact

Use: Thought to be a spark plug-like object; actual purpose unknown.

Inventors: Discovered in 1961 in California, encased in a hard rock or geode.

Modern Findings: Likely a 1920s-era Champion spark plug.

Speculations: Some speculate it as evidence of ancient advanced civilizations or time travel.

Significance: Often cited in discussions of out-of-place artifacts

Hero's Steam Engine (Aeolipile)

Use: An early example of a steam engine, primarily a novelty.

Inventors: Described by Hero of Alexandria in the 1st century AD.

Modern Findings: Operated by steam pressure generated by boiling water.

Speculations: Could have been used for practical purposes if further developed.

Significance: Represents the untapped potential of ancient technology.

Nimrud Lens

Use: Possibly used as a magnifying glass or for starting fires.

Inventors: Assyrian, dating back to the 7th century BC.

Modern Findings: Made of natural rock crystal.

Speculations: Some historians suggest it could have been part of a telescope.

Significance: One of the earliest examples of a lens in human history.

Ancient Concrete

Use: Used in Roman construction, notably in the Pantheon's dome.

Inventors: Roman engineers; unique due to the use of volcanic ash.

Modern Findings: More durable and environmentally friendly than modern concrete.

Speculations: Its enduring nature is attributed to the chemical reaction between volcanic ash and lime.

Significance: Continues to influence modern concrete research and development.

WACKY LOCATIONS

DON'T GO THERE!

 Dragon's Triangle (Devil's Sea), Japan
Located near the Japanese coast in the Pacific Ocean.
Notorious for numerous reports of vanished ships and aircraft.
Similar to the Bermuda Triangle, it's often linked to paranormal or extraterrestrial activities.
The region is also known for its underwater volcanic activity, which could explain some disappearances.
Recognized by some as a danger zone by the Japanese government.

 Superstition Mountains, Arizona, USA
Located east of Phoenix, Arizona, these mountains are infamous for the legend of the Lost Dutchman's Gold Mine.
Many adventurers and treasure hunters have gone missing while searching for the mine.
The area is rife with legends of curses and hauntings.
Challenging terrain and extreme weather conditions add to the dangers.
Native American legends warn of supernatural guardians protecting the secrets of the mountains.

49

The Sargasso Sea, Atlantic Ocean

Located in the North Atlantic, it is known for its still waters and thick seaweed.

Associated with stories of ships getting trapped and immobilized by the seaweed.

The area has a history of mysterious disappearances of vessels, akin to the Bermuda Triangle.

Unlike other regions, it has no shores and is defined by ocean currents.

Sometimes referred to as the "graveyard of ships," with several unexplained incidents reported.

The South Atlantic Anomaly

An area where the Earth's inner Van Allen radiation belt comes closest to the Earth's surface.

Known for causing problems with satellites and spacecraft, including the Hubble Space Telescope.

Sometimes referred to as the "Bermuda Triangle of space" due to its high levels of radiation.

Affects onboard computers and exposes astronauts to higher-than-usual levels of radiation.

The anomaly is slowly moving and changing, affecting different parts of space over time.

The Marysburgh Vortex, Canada
Located in Lake Ontario, this area is part of the Great Lakes Triangle.
Known for numerous shipwrecks, strange disappearances of ships and aircraft, and compass malfunctions.
Legends and reports include ghost ships, UFO sightings, and other unexplained phenomena.
The area has a history of violent storms, which may contribute to some of the disappearances.

The Bridgewater Triangle, Massachusetts, USA
An area of about 200 square miles in southeastern Massachusetts.
Known for a variety of paranormal phenomena, including UFO sightings, poltergeists, orbs, and Bigfoot-like sightings.
The area also has a history of unexplained disappearances and numerous reports of bizarre animal mutilations.
The Hockomock Swamp, located within the triangle, is central to many of these legends and is considered sacred by local Native American tribes.

04

CHAPTER

04

RENAISSANCE PERIOD

THEY COULD SEE THAT FAR?

 The Printing Press: Invented by Johannes Gutenberg around 1440, the printing press revolutionized the spread of information, making books more accessible and promoting literacy.

 Leonardo da Vinci's Notebooks: Leonardo da Vinci, a polymath, filled notebooks with over 13,000 pages of observations, inventions, and art, including designs for a helicopter, tank, and solar power.

 The Sistine Chapel Ceiling: Michelangelo's masterpiece, painted between 1508 and 1512, was a remarkable feat of artistry and physical endurance, as he worked on his back for four years to complete it.

▶▶ **Shakespeare's Influence**: William Shakespeare, active during the Renaissance's later years, contributed over 1,700 words to the English language and wrote plays that are still performed today.

▶▶ Galileo's Telescope: Galileo Galilei improved the telescope in 1609, leading to major astronomical discoveries like the moons of Jupiter, phases of Venus, and details of the moon's surface.

▶▶ The Birth of Opera: Around the turn of the 17th century, opera began in Italy, blending music, drama, and scenic design into a new form of entertainment.

▶▶ New World Maps: The Renaissance saw significant advancements in cartography. The 1507 Waldseemüller map was the first to depict and name the Americas as separate from Asia.

Renaissance Fashion: Clothing became a form of expression and status. The use of vibrant colors, luxurious materials, and elaborate designs characterized Renaissance fashion.

 Women Artists: Despite societal constraints, women like Sofonisba Anguissola and Artemisia Gentileschi became accomplished Renaissance artists.

 The Witch Hunts: The Renaissance also saw a rise in witch hunts across Europe, fueled by superstition and religious fervor, resulting in tens of thousands of executions.

 Age of Exploration: The Renaissance era overlapped with the Age of Exploration, leading to European discoveries of new lands and sea routes, like Columbus's 1492 voyage.

 Renaissance Science and Alchemy: The pursuit of alchemy, the precursor to chemistry, was common, with figures like Paracelsus making significant contributions to medicine and science.

▶▶ **Botanical Gardens**: The first botanical gardens were established in Italian universities to study medicinal plants, marking a new approach to scientific research.

▶▶ Renaissance Festivals: Festivals and tournaments were grand affairs, featuring jousting, music, and theater, reflecting the era's cultural richness. Some are still held today.

▶▶ The Spread of Coffee: Coffee, which arrived in Europe during the Renaissance, quickly became popular, leading to the opening of coffeehouses as social and intellectual hubs.

▶▶ Nicolaus Copernicus: Copernicus proposed the heliocentric model of the universe in 1543, challenging the long-held geocentric view and laying the groundwork for modern astronomy.

SCIENTIFIC REVOLUTION

FINALLY, SCIENCE!

 Advances in Various Fields: The Scientific Revolution saw advances in many areas, including astronomy, physics, biology, and chemistry. It laid the groundwork for modern science.

 The Scientific Method: Perhaps the most lasting impact was the development of the scientific method, a systematic approach to research based on hypothesis, experimentation, observation, and the formulation of theories. This method is still the foundation of scientific inquiry today.

 Laws of Motion and Universal Gravitation (Isaac Newton): Newton's Principia Mathematica (1687) laid the foundation for classical mechanics, introducing the laws of motion and the law of universal gravitation.

 Microscopy and Cell Discovery (Robert Hooke): In 1665, Hooke used a microscope to observe the structure of cork and coined the term "cell" to describe the basic unit of life.

 Blood Circulation (William Harvey): Harvey's work on the circulation of blood in 1628 overturned centuries-old beliefs about the human body and laid the foundation for modern physiology.

 Thermometer: The development of the thermometer, although not credited to a single inventor, was refined during this period, allowing for more accurate temperature measurements.

 Calculus (Isaac Newton and Gottfried Wilhelm Leibniz): Newton and Leibniz independently developed calculus, a branch of mathematics essential for describing motion and change.

Discovery of Gas Laws (Robert Boyle and Others): Boyle's law, which describes the inversely proportional relationship between the pressure and volume of a gas, was among the first physical laws to be expressed in a mathematical formula.

 Chemistry Advances (Robert Boyle, Antoine Lavoisier, and Others): The foundations of modern chemistry were laid during this period, moving away from alchemy and towards systematic scientific investigation.

 Astronomical Observations and Catalog (Tycho Brahe): Brahe made the most accurate astronomical observations of his time without a telescope and compiled a comprehensive star catalog.

 Anatomical Studies (Andreas Vesalius): Vesalius's detailed study of human anatomy, published in 1543, corrected many misconceptions and was based on direct observations from dissections.

INDUSTRIAL REVOLUTION

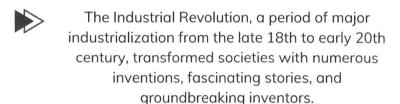

WHAT WAS IT LIKE TO LIVE IN THE AGE OF STEAM?

▶ The Industrial Revolution, a period of major industrialization from the late 18th to early 20th century, transformed societies with numerous inventions, fascinating stories, and groundbreaking inventors.

▶ Steam Engine Revolutionized by James Watt: While not the inventor of the steam engine, Watt dramatically improved its efficiency, which became a driving force of the Industrial Revolution.

▶ The Luddites: Named after Ned Ludd, the Luddites were workers who destroyed machinery, especially in textile factories, fearing it would replace their skilled labor.

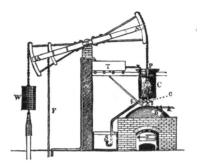

 First Passenger Railway: The world's first public passenger railway opened in 1825 between Stockton and Darlington in England.

 Child Labor: Shockingly, children as young as six worked in factories and mines under dangerous conditions during the Industrial Revolution.

 Invention of the Telegraph: Samuel Morse developed the electric telegraph in the 1830s and the Morse code, revolutionizing long-distance communication.

 Cotton Gin: Invented by Eli Whitney in 1793, the cotton gin revolutionized the cotton industry by dramatically speeding up the process of separating cotton seeds from cotton fiber.

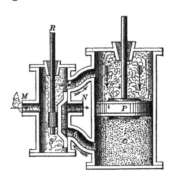

Spinning Jenny: Invented by James Hargreaves in 1764, the Spinning Jenny allowed one worker to spin several threads at once, greatly enhancing productivity in textile production.

 Vulcanization of Rubber: Charles Goodyear discovered the process of vulcanization in 1839, making rubber more durable and paving the way for the modern rubber industry.

 First Photograph: The first ever photograph was taken in 1826 by Joseph Nicéphore Niépce using a process called heliography.

 The Factory Act of 1833: This act was one of the first attempts to regulate child labor in Britain, setting minimum age limits and maximum working hours.

 Anesthesia in Surgery: The discovery and application of ether and chloroform as anesthetics in the 1840s allowed for more complex and less painful surgical procedures.

Bessemer Process: Henry Bessemer's invention in 1856 allowed for the mass production of steel, drastically reducing its cost and paving the way for its widespread use in construction and manufacturing.

 The Penny Post: In 1840, the Uniform Penny Post was established in the UK by Rowland Hill, making postal services affordable for everyday people.

 Population Shift: The Industrial Revolution led to a massive shift of population from rural areas to cities, as people moved to work in factories.

 Phonograph: Thomas Edison invented the phonograph in 1877, the first device to both record and reproduce sound.

 The Typewriter: The first practical typewriter was invented by Christopher Latham Sholes in 1868, revolutionizing office work.

 Introduction of Standard Time Zones: The need for standardized time became apparent with the advent of railroads and telegraph systems, leading to the introduction of standard time zones in the 1880s.

DIGITAL REVOLUTION

INFORMATION, A GIFT OR A CURSE?

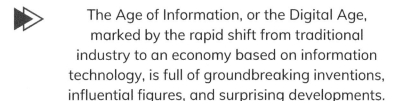

▶▶ The Age of Information, or the Digital Age, marked by the rapid shift from traditional industry to an economy based on information technology, is full of groundbreaking inventions, influential figures, and surprising developments.

▶▶ Birth of the Internet: The precursor to the internet, ARPANET, was developed in the late 1960s and early 1970s. It laid the foundation for the modern internet.

▶▶ First Email: Ray Tomlinson sent the first email in 1971, choosing the "@" symbol to designate email addresses.

▶▶ **Apple's Garage Beginnings:** Apple Inc., founded by Steve Jobs, Steve Wozniak, and Ronald Wayne, started in a garage. Their first product was the Apple I computer.

64

 Google's Algorithm: Larry Page and Sergey Brin developed the PageRank algorithm, forming the basis for Google's search engine, in a college dorm room.

 The Dot-com Bubble: The late 1990s saw a rapid rise and fall in internet-based companies, known as the dot-com bubble.

 Social Media Boom: Mark Zuckerberg launched Facebook from his Harvard dormitory room in 2004, revolutionizing social media.

 Mobile Revolution: The introduction of smartphones, particularly the iPhone in 2007, drastically changed the way people communicate and access information.

 Amazon's Evolution: Started as an online bookstore by Jeff Bezos, Amazon quickly expanded and became one of the world's largest online retailers.

Spinning Jenny: Invented by James Hargreaves in 1764, the Spinning Jenny allowed one worker to spin several threads at once, greatly enhancing productivity in textile production.

 Vulcanization of Rubber: Charles Goodyear discovered the process of vulcanization in 1839, making rubber more durable and paving the way for the modern rubber industry.

 First Photograph: The first ever photograph was taken in 1826 by Joseph Nicéphore Niépce using a process called heliography.

 The Factory Act of 1833: This act was one of the first attempts to regulate child labor in Britain, setting minimum age limits and maximum working hours.

 Anesthesia in Surgery: The discovery and application of ether and chloroform as anesthetics in the 1840s allowed for more complex and less painful surgical procedures.

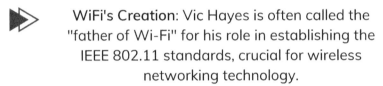 **WiFi's Creation**: Vic Hayes is often called the "father of Wi-Fi" for his role in establishing the IEEE 802.11 standards, crucial for wireless networking technology.

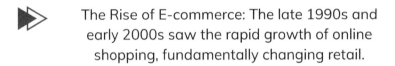 The Rise of E-commerce: The late 1990s and early 2000s saw the rapid growth of online shopping, fundamentally changing retail.

Streaming Services: Netflix transitioned from DVD rental to streaming services, revolutionizing how people consume media. Also putting many physical movie rental businesses, out of business.

Google Maps: Launched in 2005, Google Maps revolutionized navigation and location-based services. Before this, people regularly used maps to travel long distances.

05

CHAPTER

05

AMERICAN REVOLUTIONARY WAR

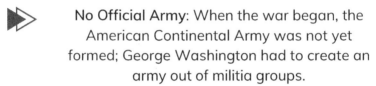

WELL, WHEN TALKING STOPS...

▶▶ **No Official Army:** When the war began, the American Continental Army was not yet formed; George Washington had to create an army out of militia groups.

▶▶ Foreign Assistance: The Americans received crucial assistance from foreign nations, most notably France, which provided supplies, troops, and naval support.

▶▶ First Submarine Attack: The Turtle, an early submarine, was used in an unsuccessful attempt to attach explosives to British ships.

▶▶ African American Soldiers: Both free and enslaved African Americans fought in the war, with some gaining freedom as a result.

 **Benjamin Franklin's Diplomacy**: Franklin's diplomacy in France was vital in securing French support for the American cause.

 Paul Revere's Ride: Paul Revere's famous midnight ride to warn of British troop movements was not a solo effort; he was joined by William Dawes and Samuel Prescott.

 American Privateers: Privateers, privately owned armed boats, played a significant role in disrupting British supply lines.

 **Oldest Commissioned Naval Vessel**: USS Constitution, nicknamed "Old Ironsides," was launched in 1797 and is the world's oldest commissioned naval vessel still afloat.

 Loyalists: Around 15-20% of the colonial population were Loyalists who supported the British Crown.

The Siege of Yorktown: The last major land battle of the American Revolution, leading to British General Cornwallis's surrender.

 Invisible Ink: Both sides used invisible ink to send secret messages.

 Native American Involvement: Many Native American tribes were involved in the war, with allegiances split between the British and Americans.

 Smallpox: Disease, particularly smallpox, killed more American soldiers than combat.

 Swamp Fox: Francis Marion, known as the "Swamp Fox," was famous for his irregular warfare tactics in South Carolina.

 Women in Combat: Women also played roles in combat; notable examples include Molly Pitcher, who manned a cannon.

THE NAPOLEONIC WARS

HE WANTED ALL THE SMOKE.

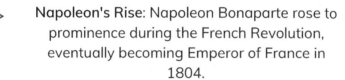

▶▶ **Napoleon's Rise:** Napoleon Bonaparte rose to prominence during the French Revolution, eventually becoming Emperor of France in 1804.

▶▶ **A Global Conflict:** The Napoleonic Wars involved most European nations and had campaigns in the Middle East, North America, and the Caribbean.

▶▶ **Battle of Trafalgar (1805):** A pivotal naval battle where British Admiral Nelson defeated the combined French and Spanish fleets. Nelson was killed in the battle.

▶▶ **Napoleon's Exile to Elba:** After his defeat in 1814, Napoleon was exiled to Elba, a small island in the Mediterranean.

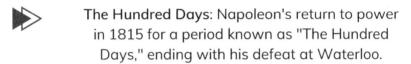

The Hundred Days: Napoleon's return to power in 1815 for a period known as "The Hundred Days," ending with his defeat at Waterloo.

Napoleon's Final Exile: After Waterloo, Napoleon was exiled to Saint Helena, where he died in 1821.

The Rosetta Stone: Discovered by French soldiers in Egypt in 1799, it was key to deciphering Egyptian hieroglyphs.

Introduction of the Metric System: The Napoleonic Wars helped spread the use of the metric system across Europe.

Napoleonic Code: Napoleon reformed French law with the Napoleonic Code, a model for legal systems in many countries.

First Use of Canister Shot: An anti-personnel artillery ammunition, which exploded mid-air to release small metal balls, increasing its lethality.

 Invention of the Ambulance: The concept of rapid medical treatment and evacuation from battlefields was developed by Napoleon's chief surgeon.

 The Louisiana Purchase (1803): France sold Louisiana to the United States, effectively doubling its size.

 Invasion of Russia (1812): Napoleon's disastrous Russian campaign resulted in the loss of over 400,000 soldiers.

 Napoleon's Height: Contrary to the popular myth of being extremely short, Napoleon was of average height for his time (5'6").

 Napoleon's Divorce: He divorced Josephine, his first wife, because she could not produce an heir. She was also quite unfaithful.

WORLD WAR 1

SO NO ONE MOVED FORWARD?

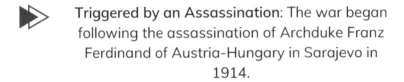 **Triggered by an Assassination:** The war began following the assassination of Archduke Franz Ferdinand of Austria-Hungary in Sarajevo in 1914.

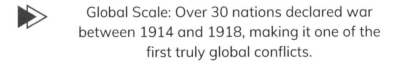 Global Scale: Over 30 nations declared war between 1914 and 1918, making it one of the first truly global conflicts.

Trench Warfare: Much of the Western Front was characterized by trench warfare. Trench warfare meant that each side would get in ditches called trenches. They would attack each other and try to gain ground. But often times, it would end in a stalemate, and neither side would advance.

First Use of Tanks: Tanks were first used in combat by the British during the Battle of the Somme in 1916.

▶▷ **The Lusitania**: The sinking of the RMS Lusitania by a German U-boat in 1915 killed 1,198 people and played a role in bringing the United States into the war.

▶▷ War of Attrition: The war became a war of attrition, with victory going to the side that could endure the longest.

▶▷ The Christmas Truce: In 1914, some German and British troops spontaneously declared a ceasefire on Christmas Day, even playing football together in no-man's land.

▶▷ No Man's Land: The area between opposing trenches was known as no-man's land, often consisting of barbed wire and mines.

Influenza Pandemic: The 1918 flu pandemic, also known as the Spanish flu, killed millions worldwide and was exacerbated by the movement of troops.

 Women in the Workforce: With many men at war, women took on roles in manufacturing, transport, and other industries, changing perceptions of women in the workforce.

 War Dogs: Dogs were used for various tasks, including carrying messages, laying telegraph wires, and detecting mines.

 Plastic Surgery: The war led to advancements in plastic surgery due to the need to treat severe facial wounds.

 Economic Impact: The war cost the participating countries a combined $186 billion and drastically altered global economies.

 Zimmermann Telegram: In 1917, a telegram from Germany to Mexico proposing an alliance against the U.S. was intercepted, further pushing the U.S. to enter the war.

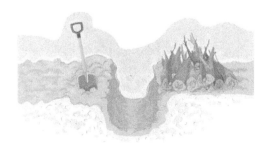

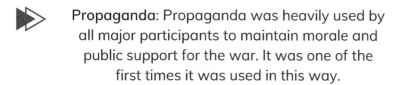 **Propaganda**: Propaganda was heavily used by all major participants to maintain morale and public support for the war. It was one of the first times it was used in this way.

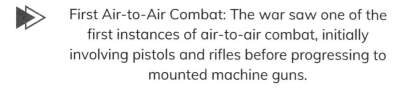 First Air-to-Air Combat: The war saw one of the first instances of air-to-air combat, initially involving pistols and rifles before progressing to mounted machine guns.

▶▷ Carrier Pigeons: Used for communication, carrier pigeons delivered important messages, with some even receiving medals for their service.

▶▷ War Poets: Poets like Wilfred Owen and Siegfried Sassoon vividly depicted the grim realities of the war in their works.

WORLD WAR 2

WHATS AN ENIGMA?

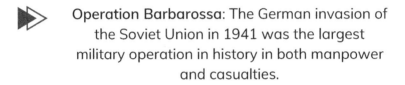 **Operation Barbarossa**: The German invasion of the Soviet Union in 1941 was the largest military operation in history in both manpower and casualties.

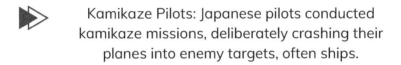 Kamikaze Pilots: Japanese pilots conducted kamikaze missions, deliberately crashing their planes into enemy targets, often ships.

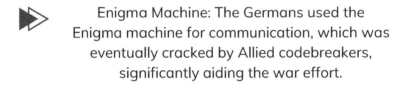 Enigma Machine: The Germans used the Enigma machine for communication, which was eventually cracked by Allied codebreakers, significantly aiding the war effort.

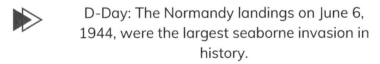 D-Day: The Normandy landings on June 6, 1944, were the largest seaborne invasion in history.

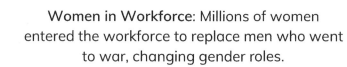

▶▶ **Women in Workforce**: Millions of women entered the workforce to replace men who went to war, changing gender roles.

▶▶ **Blitzkrieg**: The German strategy of "blitzkrieg" or "lightning war" involved rapid, coordinated assaults by air and ground forces.

▶▶ Radar: The development and use of radar were crucial for the Allies, particularly in the Battle of Britain.

▶▶ Ghost Army: The U.S. Army used a "Ghost Army" of inflatable tanks and sound effects to deceive German forces.

▶▶ Animal Heroes: Animals, including dogs, pigeons, and horses, played various roles in the war; delivering secret messages, codes, and more.

Nuremberg Trials: Post-war trials of Nazi leaders for war crimes and crimes against humanity.

 The Declaration of United Nations: The term "United Nations" was first used in 1942, leading to the formation of the United Nations in 1945.

 Children's Evacuation: Millions of children were evacuated from cities to the countryside in Britain to escape bombing raids.

 Computing Advances: The war spurred significant advances in computing, including the development of early computers like the British Colossus and the American ENIAC, which were used for calculations and code-breaking.

 Food Rationing: Many countries introduced food rationing to support the war effort.

 Manhattan Project: A secret U.S. project to develop the atomic bomb. Though many countries were developing their own atomic weapons, the united states was the first to complete this project.

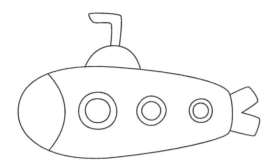

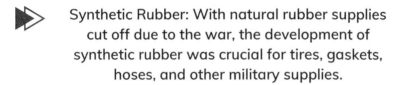

▶ Synthetic Rubber: With natural rubber supplies cut off due to the war, the development of synthetic rubber was crucial for tires, gaskets, hoses, and other military supplies.

▶ Pressurized Cabins in Aircraft: This technology allowed planes to fly at higher altitudes, above weather and enemy defenses.

▶ Napalm: Developed at Harvard University, napalm was used extensively in air raids. It was an incredibly destructive incendiary weapon. It's use however, is controversial. Some estimate napalm killed more Japanese people than the atomic bomb.

▶ Photographic Reconnaissance: High-altitude photographic reconnaissance became a crucial part of military intelligence.

▶ Duct Tape: Originally developed for sealing ammunition cases against moisture, duct tape found numerous uses both during and after the war.

THE COLD WAR

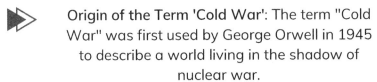

WAS THE WAR REALLY COLD?

▷▷ **Origin of the Term 'Cold War'**: The term "Cold War" was first used by George Orwell in 1945 to describe a world living in the shadow of nuclear war.

▷▷ Iron Curtain Speech: Winston Churchill's 1946 speech described an "iron curtain" descending across Europe, symbolizing the division between Western democracies and Eastern communist countries.

▷▷ Nuclear Arms Race: The U.S. and USSR competed in developing nuclear weapons, leading to a stockpile of tens of thousands of warheads.

▷▷ Cuban Missile Crisis (1962): This 13-day confrontation over Soviet missiles in Cuba was the closest the Cold War came to escalating into a full-scale nuclear war.

▶▶ **Korean War (1950-1953):** Often considered the first 'hot' conflict of the Cold War, with North Korea (backed by the USSR and China) fighting against South Korea (backed by the UN, predominantly the USA).

▶▶ Space Race: The competition between the USSR and the USA in space exploration was a key aspect of the Cold War, including the launch of Sputnik and the Apollo moon landing.

▶▶ McCarthyism: In the 1950s, U.S. Senator Joseph McCarthy led a campaign against alleged communists in the U.S., often with little evidence.

▶▶ Vietnam War: A proxy war in the larger Cold War context, where the U.S. intervened to prevent the spread of communism in South Vietnam.

NATO and the Warsaw Pact: The formation of NATO (1949) and the Warsaw Pact (1955) solidified the division between Western and Eastern military alliances.

 Berlin Wall (1961-1989): A physical and iconic symbol of the Cold War, separating East and West Berlin.

 Nuclear Submarines: The development of nuclear-powered submarines carrying ballistic missiles significantly changed naval strategy.

 Chernobyl Disaster (1986): The nuclear power plant disaster in the Soviet Union had long-lasting environmental and health impacts.

 Decolonization: Many colonies gained independence during the Cold War, often becoming battlegrounds for influence between the superpowers.

 Satellite Communications: The first communications satellite, Telstar, was launched in 1962, enabling live trans-Atlantic television broadcasts and improving global communication significantly.

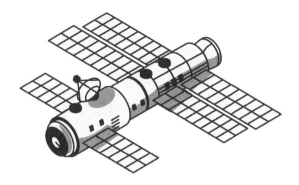

▶▷ **The Internet's Precursor:** ARPANET, developed in the late 1960s, was the forerunner of the modern internet. It initially connected several computers at universities and research labs in the U.S.

▶▷ Spy Satellites: The U.S. and the Soviet Union developed spy satellites, such as the American Corona and the Soviet Zenit series, which played crucial roles in intelligence gathering.

▶▷ Microprocessors: The development of the microprocessor in the early 1970s revolutionized the computer industry and paved the way for the development of personal computers.

▶▷ Supersonic Aircraft: Aircraft technology saw significant advancements, including the development of supersonic jets like the Concorde, which was a product of a joint venture between France and the UK.

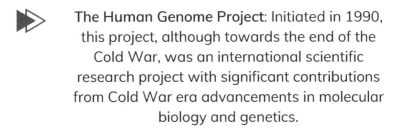 **The Human Genome Project**: Initiated in 1990, this project, although towards the end of the Cold War, was an international scientific research project with significant contributions from Cold War era advancements in molecular biology and genetics.

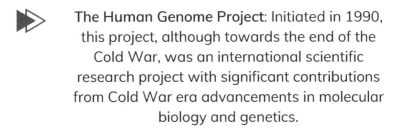 Weather Satellites: The launch of the first weather satellite, TIROS-1, in 1960, marked the beginning of the use of space-based assets to monitor Earth's weather and climate.

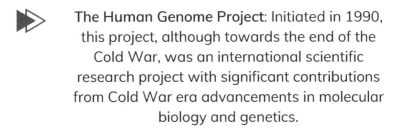 Polio Vaccine: In 1955, Jonas Salk developed the first successful polio vaccine, a significant medical breakthrough.

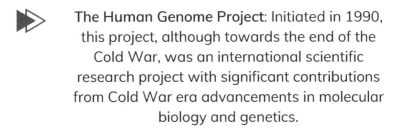 The Global Positioning System (GPS): The development of GPS began in the 1970s as a military navigation system.

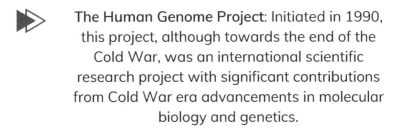 Kevlar: This high-strength synthetic fiber, known for its use in ballistic vests and helmets, was developed by Stephanie Kwolek at DuPont in 1965.

06

CHAPTER

06

AFRICAN MYTHOLOGY

WAS THE MYSTERY REALLY THAT SERIOUS?

 Anansi the Spider: In Akan folklore, Anansi is a trickster spider who can shape-shift into a human. He is a significant character in West African and Caribbean folklore.

 Yoruba Pantheon: The Yoruba people have a rich mythology with over 400 gods, known as Orishas.

 Mami Wata: A water spirit in African and African American folklore, often depicted as a mermaid or snake charmer and associated with healing and fertility.

 The Dogon and Sirius B: The Dogon tribe in Mali has myths about the Sirius star system, including detailed knowledge of its invisible companion star, Sirius B, which is invisible to the naked eye. They have had this knowledge for hundreds of years.

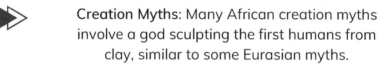

▶▷ **Creation Myths:** Many African creation myths involve a god sculpting the first humans from clay, similar to some Eurasian myths.

▶▷ Olorun and the Chain: In Yoruba mythology, the god Olorun lowered a chain from the heavens, and the god Orunmila climbed down it to create the earth.

▶▷ Sundiata Keita: The founder of the Mali Empire, Sundiata Keita, is a legendary figure whose life has become a mix of history and myth.

▶▷ The Rainbow Snake: In many African cultures, the rainbow is seen as a manifestation of a divine, benevolent snake god.

▶▷ The San and the Moon: The San people of Southern Africa believe that the moon is a man who angered the Sun, who then threw him into the sky.

The San People's Creation Myth: In this myth, a bee carried a mantis across a river; the mantis transformed into the first human.

 Ngai: The Kikuyu people of Kenya believe in a supreme god, Ngai, who resides on Mount Kenya. This is similar to the Zues in Greek Myths.

 The Senufo and Kolotyolo: The Senufo people of West Africa believe in a cosmic serpent, Kolotyolo, which is involved in the creation.

 Wagadu and the Golden Snake: According to Soninke mythology, the ancient city of Wagadu (or Ghana Empire) was protected by a serpent deity named Bida. Bida demanded a human sacrifice in exchange for ensuring prosperity, but was eventually killed, leading to the city's downfall.

 The Legend of Queen of Sheba: In Ethiopian mythology, the Queen of Sheba is known as Makeda, who visited King Solomon. Their union led to the birth of Menelik I, the founder of the Solomonic dynasty in Ethiopia.

GREEK MYTHOLOGY

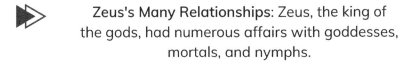

THE KING OF TOXIC BEHAVIOR!

▶▶ **Zeus's Many Relationships:** Zeus, the king of the gods, had numerous affairs with goddesses, mortals, and nymphs.

▶▶ **Athena's Birth:** Athena, goddess of wisdom, was born fully armed from Zeus's forehead.

▶▶ **Arachne's Challenge:** Arachne, a mortal woman, challenged Athena to a weaving contest and was turned into a spider for her hubris.

▶▶ **Hermes's Ingenuity:** Hermes, the messenger god, invented the lyre using a tortoise shell on the day he was born.

▶▶ **Dionysus's Dual Nature:** Dionysus, the god of wine, represents both the joy and the brutality of intoxication.

92

 The First Woman: Pandora, the first mortal woman, opened a jar (often mistranslated as a box) releasing all evils into the world.

 The Endless Punishments: Sisyphus, Tantalus, and Ixion endured eternal punishments in the Underworld for their sins against the gods.

 Achilles's Heel: Achilles was invulnerable except for his heel, where his mother Thetis held him while dipping him in the River Styx.

 The Original Marathon: Pheidippides, a messenger, ran from Marathon to Athens to announce the Greek victory over Persia, inspiring the modern marathon race.

 Hercules's Twelve Labors: Hercules, a demi-god, performed twelve labors as penance for killing his family under Hera's curse.

 Narcissus's Self-Love: Narcissus fell in love with his own reflection, leading to his demise, and giving rise to the term narcissism.

 The Creation of Man: According to Hesiod, Prometheus created man from clay, while Athena breathed life into the clay figure.

 Prometheus's Punishment: For stealing fire from the gods and giving it to humanity, Prometheus was chained to a rock where an eagle ate his liver daily.

 The Amazons: The Amazons were a tribe of warrior women who played a prominent role in various myths, including the labors of Hercules and the Trojan War.

 Cronus Ate His Children: To prevent them from overthrowing him, Cronus, the Titan father of Zeus, ate his own children. They were later saved by Zeus.

HINDU MYTHOLOGY

HOW MANY HEADS DID HE HAVE?

 Brahma's Five Heads: Originally, Brahma had five heads. Shiva cut off one because Brahma lied, leaving him with four.

 Vishnu's Ten Avatars: Vishnu has ten avatars, including Rama, Krishna, and Buddha, to maintain cosmic order.

 Shiva's Third Eye: Shiva's third eye can destroy things when opened. It's usually closed, representing a state of detachment.

 Ganesha's Elephant Head: Ganesha, the god of beginnings, was beheaded by Shiva and then given an elephant's head. This may be a pattern.

 Vimanas: Vimanas are mythological flying palaces or chariots described in ancient Hindu texts and epics, often interpreted as ancient flying machines. Some speculate they looked like UFO's.

 Brahmastra: A supernatural weapon, said to be created by Brahma, with destructive power akin to a nuclear weapon. It's mentioned in various Hindu texts.

 The Concept of Multiverse: Ancient Hindu cosmology suggests the existence of a multiverse, with multiple universes contained like bubbles in a foam.

 Chandra's 27 Wives: The moon god Chandra has 27 wives, representing the 27 lunar mansions or Nakshatras.

▶▷ **The City of Dwarka:** Krishna's city, Dwarka, is described as a grand and beautiful city and is considered by some to have been a real city that submerged under the sea.

▶▷ The Cosmic Egg: Hindu cosmology speaks of the universe as a cosmic egg, Brahmanda, which splits into two to form the heavens and the earth.

▶▷ Rishi Dadhichi's Bones: The sage Dadhichi sacrificed his life by giving his bones to make weapons (Vajra) to defeat demons.

▶▷ Hanuman's Son, Makardhwaja: Hanuman's son, Makardhwaja, was born to a fish who consumed a drop of Hanuman's sweat.

▶▷ The Four Yugas: Hindu cosmology divides time into four epochs or Yugas: Satya, Treta, Dvapara, and Kali, each with distinct characteristics and durations. These four yugas repeat themselves in a cosmic, time-cycle.

BUDDHIST MYTHOLOGY

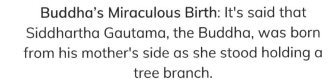

COOLIST BIRTH EVER?

▶▶ **Buddha's Miraculous Birth**: It's said that Siddhartha Gautama, the Buddha, was born from his mother's side as she stood holding a tree branch.

▶▶ **The Buddha's First Steps**: Legend states that upon his birth, Buddha took seven steps and at each step, a lotus flower appeared.

▶▶ Avalokiteshvara's Thousand Arms: Avalokiteshvara, the Bodhisattva of Compassion, is often depicted with a thousand arms, each hand with an eye, to see and help the suffering beings.

▶▶ Buddha's Long Hair: After renouncing his princely life, Buddha cut his hair, which is said to have spiraled into tight curls.

 Maitreya, the Future Buddha: Maitreya is believed to be a future Buddha who will appear on Earth, achieve complete enlightenment, and teach the pure dharma.

 The Buddha's Prediction of His Death: The Buddha predicted his own death and attained Parinirvana (final deathless state) lying between two Sal trees.

 Buddha's Daily Routine: The Buddha was known for his strict daily routine, which included periods of meditation, teaching, and rest.

 The Relics of Buddha: After his cremation, Buddha's relics were divided among his followers and enshrined in stupas.

 Buddha's Renunciation: Buddha left his royal life after encountering an old man, a sick man, a corpse, and a monk, which made him aware of life's sufferings.

 Buddha's First Sermon: His first sermon, "Setting in Motion the Wheel of Dharma," was given in Sarnath, India.

 The Hungry Tigress Jataka Tale: In a previous life, the Buddha sacrificed himself to feed a starving tigress and her cubs.

 The Mountains of Meru: Mount Meru is a sacred mountain in Buddhist, Hindu, and Jain cosmology, considered the center of all physical, metaphysical, and spiritual universes.

 The Six Realms of Existence: Buddhism describes six realms of rebirth and existence: gods, demigods, humans, animals, ghosts, and hell beings.

AZTEC MYTHOLOGY

YOU NEED WAHT TO GO ON YOUR JOURNEY?

 Dual Gods: Many Aztec gods had dual aspects, like Quetzalcoatl, who was both the god of wind and a creator deity.

 Five Suns: The Aztecs believed in five ages, or "Suns," each ended by a catastrophe. We are currently in the Fifth Sun.

 Human Heart Sacrifices: The Aztecs are well-known for their human sacrifices, especially heart extractions, to appease and nourish the gods.

 Tonatiuh, the Sun God: The Aztecs believed that the journey of the sun was enabled by the sacrifice of Tonatiuh, requiring constant nourishment by blood.

 The Feathered Serpent: Quetzalcoatl, a prominent deity, was depicted as a feathered serpent, a symbol of earth-bound things and the heavens.

 Aztec Creation Myth: The gods created humans by stealing bones from the underworld and sprinkling them with their own blood.

 Tlaloc, God of Rain: Tlaloc required the tears of the young as part of his offerings, leading to child sacrifices.

 Mictlan, the Underworld: The Aztec underworld, ruled by Mictlantecuhtli and his wife Mictecacihuatl, was a place where all the dead went, regardless of how they lived.

 The 260-Day Calendar: The Aztec calendar, Tonalpohualli, had 260 days and was used for divination.

 The Five Directions: Aztec cosmology included the four cardinal directions plus the center, each associated with different god.

 Tezcatlipoca's Smoking Mirror: Tezcatlipoca, a powerful god of night, magic, and prophecy, carried a mirror that could reveal the future and show visions.

 The Sun Stone or Aztec Calendar: Often mistaken for a calendar, the Sun Stone is actually a ceremonial basalt disk that depicts the five consecutive worlds of the sun from Aztec mythology.

 The Role of Omens: Aztecs believed in signs and omens; the birth of a two-headed animal, an eclipse, or a comet could be interpreted as messages or warnings from the gods.

ABORIGINAL MYTHOLOGY

▶▶ **Dreamtime**: Dreamtime is the Aboriginal understanding of the world, its creation, and its great stories.

▶▶ **Rainbow Serpent**: A key figure in many stories, the Rainbow Serpent is often seen as a creator god and a symbol of fertility.

▶▶ **Songlines**: These are paths across the land (or sky) which mark the route followed by 'creator-beings' during the Dreaming.

▶▶ Wandjina: These are cloud and rain spirits from the Kimberley region, known for their distinctive depictions in rock art.

▶▶ The Flying Foxes: In some stories, flying foxes (bats) carry messages between humans and the spirit world.

104

▶▶ **The Seven Sisters (The Pleiades):** A group of stars that are often depicted in stories and art, usually as a group of women being pursued by a man represented by the Orion constellation.

▶▶ The Great Flood: Similar to other cultures, some Aboriginal stories talk about a great flood that once covered the land.

▶▶ Gulaga, the Sacred Mountain: In the mythology of the Yuin people, Gulaga Mountain and her two sons (mountains) were formed in the Dreaming.

▶▶ The Moon Man: In some stories, the Moon Man, often a mischievous or malevolent figure, controls the tides and weather.

▶▶ The Milky Way: Often seen as a river in the sky, a place where spirits of the deceased go.

ZOROASTRIANISM MYTHOLOGY

IT'S OK, I LIKE FIRE TOO.

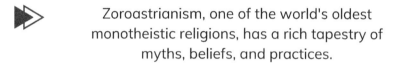

▶▶ Zoroastrianism, one of the world's oldest monotheistic religions, has a rich tapestry of myths, beliefs, and practices.

▶▶ Founded by Prophet Zoroaster: Zoroastrianism was founded by Zoroaster (or Zarathustra) in ancient Iran, approximately in the 6th century BCE.

▶▶ Ahura Mazda: The supreme god in Zoroastrianism, representing all that is good, just, and wise.

▶▶ Angra Mainyu: The destructive spirit and the adversary of Ahura Mazda, representing evil, chaos, and disorder.

▶▶ Fire Temples: Fire is a central symbol in Zoroastrian worship, and temples often house a continually burning flame.

 The Chinvat Bridge: After death, souls must cross this bridge to reach the afterlife. The righteous pass easily, but the wicked find it as narrow as a razor's edge.

 Fravashis: Guardian spirits that guide and protect individuals, families, and even physical places.

 Amesha Spentas: The seven Holy Immortals, divine beings created by Ahura Mazda, each representing an aspect of creation and a moral quality.

 Zoroaster's Miraculous Birth: Legend says that Zoroaster laughed upon being born, and his birth was accompanied by supernatural phenomena.

 Ritual Cleanliness: Purity, especially concerning fire and water, is crucial in Zoroastrian practice.

CHAPTER

07

07

ATLANTIS: FACT OR MYTH

DID IT REALLY EXIST?

▷▷ **Origin in Plato's Dialogues**: Atlantis first appears in Plato's dialogues "Timaeus" and "Critias," written around 360 BC. These are the only known ancient sources that directly mention Atlantis.

▷▷ **Described as a Large Island**: In Plato's account, Atlantis was a large island located beyond the "Pillars of Hercules," commonly believed to be the Strait of Gibraltar.

▷▷ **Advanced Civilization**: Atlantis was described as a technologically advanced and highly sophisticated civilization. It was said to have impressive architecture, complex engineering, and a powerful army and navy.

▷▷ **The Atlantean Society**: According to Plato, the society of Atlantis was a utopian blend of technology and nature, with a focus on harmony and engineering marvels.

108

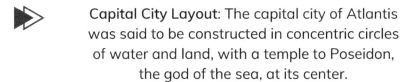

▶ **Capital City Layout**: The capital city of Atlantis was said to be constructed in concentric circles of water and land, with a temple to Poseidon, the god of the sea, at its center.

▶ Downfall and Destruction: Plato tells that the Atlanteans became morally corrupt over time, leading the gods to become angry and eventually causing the island to sink into the sea in a single day and night of misfortune.

▶ Location Theories: The exact location of Atlantis remains a topic of debate, with theories ranging from the Mediterranean Sea to the Caribbean, Antarctica, and even the idea that it was a metaphorical rather than a physical place.

▶ Archaeological and Historical Debate: Despite extensive searches and various hypotheses, no definitive archaeological evidence has been found to confirm the existence of Atlantis. It remains a subject of historical and archaeological speculation and debate.

KNIGHTS OF THE ROUND TABLE

I NEVER KNEW THAT ABOUT ROUND TABLES!

 Legendary Origin: The Knights of the Round Table originate from Arthurian legends, medieval stories about the legendary King Arthur and his knights. These stories were popular in medieval Europe and continue to be well-known today.

 Symbol of Equality: The Round Table was symbolic of equality and unity among Arthur's knights. Unlike a traditional rectangular table where the king would sit at the head, a round table had no head, indicating that all who sat there had equal status.

 Famous Knights: Some of the most famous knights include Sir Lancelot, Sir Gawain, Sir Galahad, Sir Percival, and Sir Tristan. Each knight had his own set of stories, adventures, and attributes that contributed to the legend.

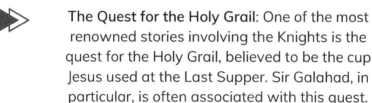 **The Quest for the Holy Grail:** One of the most renowned stories involving the Knights is the quest for the Holy Grail, believed to be the cup Jesus used at the Last Supper. Sir Galahad, in particular, is often associated with this quest.

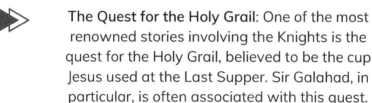 Camelot: Camelot was the castle and court associated with King Arthur. It served as the meeting place for the Knights of the Round Table and was the center of Arthur's kingdom.

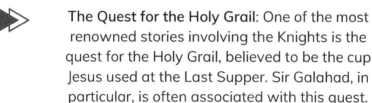 Women in Arthurian Legends: While the Round Table was predominantly male, there are stories of female knights or warriors who interacted with or were part of Arthur's court, like the Lady of the Lake.

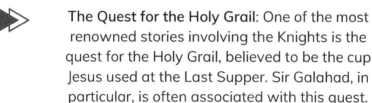 Literary Evolution: The legend of the Knights of the Round Table evolved over centuries, with contributions from various authors such as Geoffrey of Monmouth, Chrétien de Troyes, and Sir Thomas Malory, each adding their own elements and stories to the legend.

THE BLACK DEATH:

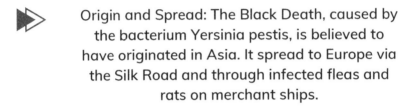 **Origin and Spread:** The Black Death, caused by the bacterium Yersinia pestis, is believed to have originated in Asia. It spread to Europe via the Silk Road and through infected fleas and rats on merchant ships.

Peak Period: The pandemic reached its peak in Europe between 1347 and 1351, devastating the continent's population.

Death Toll: It is estimated that the Black Death killed about 25 million people in Europe alone, which was about 30% to 60% of the European population at the time.

Symptoms: Victims of the Black Death suffered from symptoms such as high fever, chills, vomiting, diarrhea, terrible aches and pains— and then, in short order, death. Buboes, or swollen lymph nodes, were a characteristic symptom, often appearing in the armpits and groin.

112

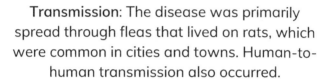

▷▷ **Transmission**: The disease was primarily spread through fleas that lived on rats, which were common in cities and towns. Human-to-human transmission also occurred.

▷▷ **Social and Economic Impact**: The Black Death had a profound impact on Europe's social structure and economy. With the high death toll, labor became scarce, leading to better wages for workers and the decline of the feudal system.

▷▷ **Religious Impact**: The pandemic led to a rise in religious extremism and persecution. Many people believed the Black Death was a punishment from God, leading to increased religiosity and, in some cases, persecution of groups such as Jews, whom they irrationally blamed for the plague.

▷▷ Reoccurrences: The Black Death wasn't a one-time event; it reoccurred in various waves over the centuries. The last significant outbreak in Europe was the Great Plague of London in 1665-1666.

mARCO POLO

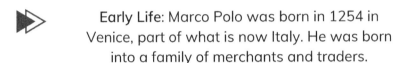 **Early Life**: Marco Polo was born in 1254 in Venice, part of what is now Italy. He was born into a family of merchants and traders.

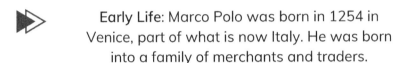 **The Journey to Asia**: In 1271, at the age of 17, Marco Polo embarked on an epic journey to Asia along with his father and uncle, Niccolò and Maffeo Polo, who were also merchants.

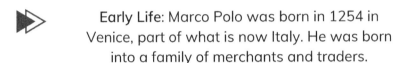 **The Court of Kublai Khan**: The Polos reached the court of Kublai Khan, the Mongol ruler of China and the grandson of Genghis Khan. Marco became a favorite of the Khan, who appointed him to high posts in his administration.

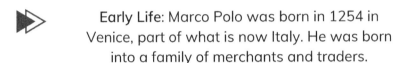 **Extensive Travels**: Marco Polo traveled extensively in the Mongol Empire, which covered much of Asia. He is believed to have journeyed through regions that are now part of modern-day China, India, Tibet, and Southeast Asia.

114

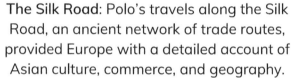

▷▷ **The Silk Road**: Polo's travels along the Silk Road, an ancient network of trade routes, provided Europe with a detailed account of Asian culture, commerce, and geography.

▷▷ **The Travels of Marco Polo'**: After returning to Venice, Marco Polo was captured during a conflict with the rival city-state of Genoa. While in prison, he dictated an account of his travels to a fellow inmate, Rustichello da Pisa, which became known as "Il Milione" or "The Travels of Marco Polo."

▷▷ **Descriptions of the East**: His book offered one of the first comprehensive looks into the Eastern world for Europeans, including descriptions of China's wealth, paper money, and the use of coal as a fuel.

▷▷ **Cultural Exchange**: Marco Polo's accounts are credited with inspiring other explorers, including Christopher Columbus, and contributing significantly to East-West cultural exchange.

 Legacy: Marco Polo is remembered as one of the world's greatest explorers. His journey was one of the earliest recorded examples of East meeting West, and his detailed accounts opened up a new world of knowledge and understanding for Europeans.

 Skepticism About His Accounts: Many modern historians and scholars express skepticism about the accuracy of Marco Polo's descriptions. Some argue that his accounts were exaggerated or romanticized, while others speculate that he may not have traveled as extensively as he claimed, or even reached China at all. This skepticism is fueled by the lack of detailed descriptions of certain aspects of Chinese life (such as the Great Wall or the practice of foot binding) and inconsistencies in his narrations. Additionally, some of the places and events Polo described have not been corroborated by other sources. Despite these doubts, his book remains a valuable historical document, offering a unique perspective on the medieval world.

THE MYSTERY OF ROANOKE ISLAND

IMAGINE COMING HOME, AND EVERYONE IS GONE!

▷ **Establishment of the Colony:** Roanoke Island, located in present-day North Carolina, was the site of the Roanoke Colony established in 1587, sponsored by Sir Walter Raleigh. It was the first English settlement in the New World.

▷ **John White's Leadership:** The colony was led by John White, an artist and friend of Raleigh, who was appointed as the governor. He played a critical role in the colony's history.

▷ **Difficult Beginnings:** The settlers arrived late in the planting season, which made the food supply and survival challenging. They were reliant on supplies from England and the goodwill of the native tribes.

▷ **Native American Relations:** Initial relations with the local Native American tribes were mixed. While there were friendly interactions, tensions and mistrust also existed, partly due to previous expeditions and confrontations.

117

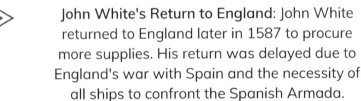

John White's Return to England: John White returned to England later in 1587 to procure more supplies. His return was delayed due to England's war with Spain and the necessity of all ships to confront the Spanish Armada.

The Mysterious Disappearance: When White finally returned in 1590, the colony was deserted with no sign of struggle or battle. The only clue was the word "CROATOAN" carved into a post and "CRO" carved into a tree.

Croatoan – A Clue?: Croatoan was the name of a nearby island (modern-day Hatteras Island) and also the name of a Native American tribe. It's believed this could have been a clue left by the colonists indicating their destination.

Archaeological Investigations: Modern archaeological efforts have uncovered some artifacts that might be linked to the Roanoke settlers, but a definitive conclusion about the fate of the colony remains elusive.

VLAD
THE
IMPALER

HE DID WHAT????

▶▶ **Historical Reign:** Vlad the Impaler ruled Wallachia at various times from 1448 to 1476. His reign was marked by frequent battles against the Ottomans and internal political rivals.

▶▶ **Early Life:** Born in 1431 in the Kingdom of Hungary (now part of Romania), Vlad was the second son of Vlad Dracul, a member of the Order of the Dragon, which was devoted to halting the Ottoman advance into Europe.

▶▶ **Nickname and the Order of the Dragon:** The name "Dracula" comes from his father's title, Dracul, meaning "Dragon" in Romanian. Dracula means "son of the Dragon." The association with the legendary vampire Count Dracula came much later, through literature.

119

 Political Hostage: As a young boy, Vlad and his brother Radu were held as political hostages by the Ottoman Empire to ensure their father's loyalty. This experience had a significant impact on Vlad's rule and his attitude towards the Ottomans.

 Reputation for Cruelty: Vlad III earned the nickname "Tepes" (Impaler) because of his preferred method of execution—impaling his enemies on stakes. This method was notoriously brutal and served as a warning to others.

 Defensive Tactics against Ottomans: Vlad is credited with using guerrilla tactics and psychological warfare in his resistance against the Ottomans. His most infamous act was the night attack in 1462, where he attempted to assassinate Sultan Mehmed II.

▶▶ **The Forest of the Impaled:** After an Ottoman army approached his capital of Târgoviște, they found it deserted except for a forest of the impaled, with over 20,000 victims. This gruesome sight demoralized the Ottomans and became infamous throughout Europe.

▶▶ **Legacy in Romania:** In Romania, Vlad is often viewed as a hero who resisted Ottoman domination. His rule is remembered for its fierce assertion of independence and justice, albeit through harsh methods.

▶▶ **Cultural Legacy:** Vlad the Impaler became a significant figure in popular culture, largely due to Bram Stoker's 1897 novel "Dracula," which loosely based its titular character on Vlad. This association cemented Vlad's place as a legendary, albeit dark, historical figure.

THE WRIGHT BROTHERS

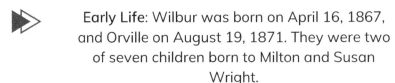

FLY, FLY AWAY!

▶▶ **Early Life**: Wilbur was born on April 16, 1867, and Orville on August 19, 1871. They were two of seven children born to Milton and Susan Wright.

▶▶ **Education**: Neither brother received a formal high school diploma, yet they were exceptionally inquisitive and well-read, learning a great deal on their own.

▶▶ **Initial Business Venture**: Before aviation, the Wright brothers started a successful bicycle repair and sales business in Dayton, Ohio, which funded their aviation experiments.

▶▶ Inspiration: Their interest in flight was inspired partly by the death of the famous German glider pilot, Otto Lilienthal, in 1896.

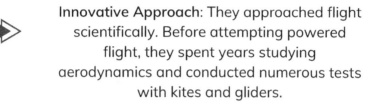 **Innovative Approach**: They approached flight scientifically. Before attempting powered flight, they spent years studying aerodynamics and conducted numerous tests with kites and gliders.

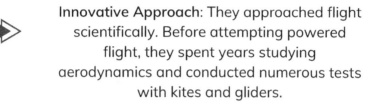 **First Controlled Flight**: On December 17, 1903, near Kitty Hawk, North Carolina, they achieved the first controlled, powered, heavier-than-air flight. Orville piloted the first flight which lasted 12 seconds.

Public Demonstrations: In 1908, they began public demonstrations of their flying machines in the United States and France, gaining international fame.

Establishing a Company: In 1909, they formed the Wright Company to produce and sell their airplanes.

Legacy and Death: Wilbur died of typhoid fever in 1912, and Orville sold the company in 1915. Orville passed away in 1948. Their legacy is immense, laying the foundation for modern aviation as we know it.

THE GREAT EMU WAR

 Background: The Great Emu War was not a traditional war, but rather a wildlife management military operation undertaken in Australia in late 1932.

 Location: This event occurred in the Campion district of Western Australia, which was experiencing significant agricultural difficulties.

 Emu Invasion: After the First World War, Australian soldiers and British veterans were given land to farm. However, they struggled with the harsh conditions. Things worsened when about 20,000 emus migrated into the area, ravaging the farmland.

 Farmers' Plight: The emus consumed and spoiled the crops, leaving the already struggling farmers in dire straits. These farmers, many of whom were veterans, appealed to the government for assistance.

124

▶▶ **Military Involvement**: In response to the farmers' pleas, the Australian government deployed a small military force equipped with two Lewis machine guns and 10,000 rounds of ammunition.

▶▶ **The Operation Begins**: The operation started in November 1932 under the command of Major G.P.W. Meredith. The soldiers quickly found that the emus were surprisingly resilient and difficult targets.

▶▶ **Challenges Faced**: The emus, being fast and agile, proved hard to kill. Even machine gun fire often only wounded the birds, which would then run off and likely die or recover later, out of sight.

▶▶ **Outcome and Withdrawal**: By December 1932, the military withdrew after two attempts, having spent thousands of rounds of ammunition with little effect on the emu population.

FOR BEING A PART OF OUR JOURNEY AND FOR
CHOOSING US AS YOUR GO-TO DESTINATION. FOR
BOOKS. WE LOOK FORWARD TO CONTINUING TO
PROVIDE YOU WITH EXCEPTIONAL LEARNING
EXPERIENCES. IF YOU GET THE OPPORTUNITY,
PLEASE LET US KNOW WHAT YOU THINK OF OUR
BOOK BY LEAVING AN AMAZON REVIEW. IT PROVIDES
US WITH THE OPPORTUNITY TO IMPROVE AND HELPS
US TO CONTINUE TO MAKE GREAT BOOKS FOR YOU.
WE TRULY APPRECIATE IT.

Made in the USA
Coppell, TX
07 November 2024

39804213R00075